# START-UP
# CITIZENSHIP

# MAKING CHOICES

## Louise and Richard Spilsbury

Evans

Published by Evans Brothers Limited
2A Portman Mansions
Chiltern Street
London W1U 6NR

© Evans Brothers Limited 2007

Produced for Evans Brothers Limited by
White-Thomson Publishing Ltd.
Bridgewater Business Centre, 210 High Street,
Lewes, East Sussex BN7 2NH

Printed in China by WKT Co. Ltd.

Editor: Clare Collinson
Consultant: Roy Honeybone, Consultant in Citizenship
Education and Editor of *Teaching Citizenship*, the
journal of the Association for Citizenship Teaching
Designer: Leishman Design

British Library Cataloguing in Publication Data
Spilsbury, Louise
 Making Choices : Louise Spilsbury, Richard
 Spilsbury. - (Start-up Citizenship)
 1. Choice (Psychology) - Juvenile literature 2.
 Ethics - Juvenile literature 3. Citizenship - Juvenile
 Literature
 I. Title II. Spilsbury, Richard, 1963-
 170

ISBN13: 9780237532635

**Acknowledgements:**
Special thanks to the following for their help and
involvement in the preparation of this book: staff, pupils
and parents at Holyoakes Field First School, Redditch,
Matchborough First School, Redditch and Mount
Carmel RC First School, Redditch.

**Picture Acknowledgements:**
Alamy p. 12 (Travel Ink); Martyn Chillmaid pp. 4
(both), 5l, 6 (both), 7, 10 (all), 11 (both), 13, title page
and 14, 15, 16, 17, 19, 21l; Corbis p. 5r (Paul Barton);
Getty Images p. 18tr ((Teubner Foodfoto);
iStockphoto.com pp. 8, 18l, 18br, 21r; London Borough
of Bromley p. 9.

**Artwork:**
Hattie Spilsbury pp. 13, 20.

# Contents

# Making choices

We all make choices all of the time. When we decide which clothes to wear or which colour pen to use we make a choice. We make some choices based on what we like or dislike.

"I choose books about animals because I like animals."

"I don't have eggs for breakfast because I don't like them."

What choices have you made today?

choices    decide    like    dislike

We make some choices based on what we know is **right** or **wrong**. Can you think of examples of right and wrong choices?

▲ What is the right thing to do with our litter?

▲ Has this boy chosen the right safety gear for rollerblading?

right   wrong   litter

# How do we make choices?

Sometimes we have several options. How do we work out which is the right option to choose?

▲ Sam's mum is helping him to choose a club to join.

▲ Jake's dad is checking the weather forecast to help the family choose a day trip.

options

Our choices may affect other people. This means we have a **responsibility** to think what they want as well.

▲ This class is **discussing** playground choices. They agree to play football at lunchtime on Mondays, Wednesdays and Fridays. Then the playground will be free for other games on Tuesdays and Thursdays.

**responsibility     discussing**

# Changing choices

Some of our choices affect the environment, or the world around us.

▲ Travelling by car causes lots of fumes. Car fumes cause air pollution.

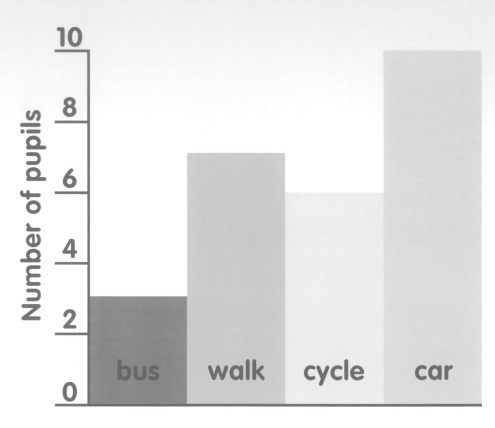

▲ Jack's class does a survey to find out how children get to school. How do most of the children get to school?

environment pollution survey

The children discuss alternative ways of getting to school. Some people choose to go by bus. Others share car trips. Some children start a walking bus. They walk to school together with an adult on a safe route.

"We like the walking bus because it gives us a chance to chat to friends on the way to school."

Why is walking to school a healthy choice?

alternative    share    walking bus

# Money matters

Do you get pocket money? What do you choose to buy with it? Do you **save** any of it?

Imagine you have £3 to spend. Choose something to eat or drink and something to play with from this picture. How much did you spend? How much **change** do you have?

£1.50

60p

£1.20

40p

£1.00

60p

£1.50

£1.20

save   change

Callum's class has a **budget** for a school trip. In groups the children choose where they want to go.

◀ Callum **explains** his group's choice to the class.

► How do the children **vote** for their choice of trip? Is this a **fair** way of choosing? How else could they have voted?

**budget    explains    vote    fair    11**

# Influences

There are many influences that affect our choices and decisions. Have you ever chosen some food or a toy because you saw it in an advert? Adverts often affect our choices.

◄ There are adverts on the television, in shops and in magazines. Where else do we see adverts? Why are these places chosen?

influences   decisions   advert

► Meg and Daisy are talking about some adverts they have cut out from magazines. What adverts do you like? Why? How do adverts try to persuade us to buy things?

Try new Stars cereal
It's the Best!

STARS
CEREAL

FUN SHAPES
AND
YUMMY
TOO

FREE
GIFT!

And it is good for you too!

◄ Meg and Daisy make their own poster for a cereal. What words have they used to persuade people to choose their cereal? How would you improve the poster?

persuade    poster    improve

# Friends and choices

What makes a good friend? How can friends influence our choices? Sometimes pressure from friends can affect the choices we make.

◀ Gregory has promised his mum he will get home by 6 o'clock. Harry asks him to stay a bit longer. What should Gregory do?

Has a friend ever persuaded you to make a wrong choice? What were the consequences?

pressure    consequences

It can be hard to say no to a friend. But you always have a choice and sometimes it is important to say no.

▲ Amy's class is using role-play to practise saying no. Amy pretends a friend wants her to do something that she doesn't want to do. Should Amy explain why she doesn't want to do what her friend asks?

role-play    pretends

# Keeping safe

If you take risks you might get hurt. You can make choices to avoid danger and keep yourself safe. How does choosing to wear a helmet keep you safe when cycling?

▶ Ellie's class discuss being safe when they play. They decide to write a set of safety rules. What rules would you add to this list?

Be safe when you play
1. Never play near railway lines or lakes
2. Stay with your

risks    danger    rules

▲ A hazard is something that could be dangerous. In this kitchen there are several hazards. What things would you change to make this kitchen safe for a toddler? Can you explain your choices?

hazard    toddler

# Being healthy

The food you choose to eat and drink makes a big difference to your health. What kind of food do you like?

▶ Which of these three meals would you choose for lunch? Are these healthy meals? Why?

How can you find out which foods are healthy and which are not? Why shouldn't we eat too many sugary foods and drinks?

health    sugary

To be healthy we need to choose to be active. Being active keeps you fit.

◄ Which of these things help to keep you fit and healthy? Which do not keep you active?

What other things can you choose to do to help you stay fit and healthy? What active things do you choose to do every day?

active    fit

# Step by step

Some choices are tricky and you need to think about them carefully.

► Amir made this decision diagram to help him make choices. What do the arrows mean? What would you put on a decision diagram like this?

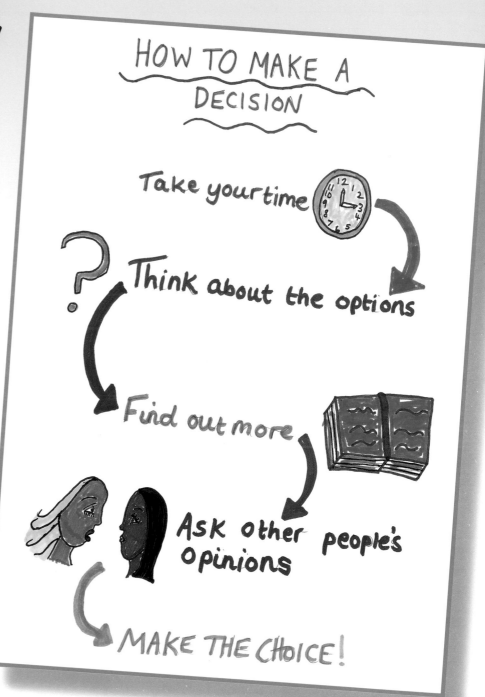

HOW TO MAKE A DECISION

Take your time

? Think about the options

Find out more

Ask other people's opinions

MAKE THE CHOICE!

diagram    arrows

How do you feel when you consider or look back at choices you have made? Which were good choices? Which were bad? How will this help your decision-making in the future?

"Next time I will think about how my choices affect other people."

"I am going to remember that I always have a right to choose and that I am allowed to change my mind!"

consider    decision-making    future    21

# Further information for

## Possible Activities

### PAGES 4-5

Children may need help recognising that they make a lot of choices in their lives. They could write a diary of what choices they make in a day. Or they could produce a class display showing their likes and dislikes. In pairs or small groups, children could come up with a list of right and wrong choices and then ask other groups to say what the right choice in each scenario is. It is important to realise that we don't always like the right choice (for example, the time it is right to choose to go to bed, which could be just when a favourite television programme is coming on!).

### PAGES 6-7

The children should understand that to be able to make the right choice we sometimes need more information about our options. They could suggest dilemmas they might face and say who they would go to for help. Encourage them to think of situations where more information is needed.

### PAGES 8-9

It is important that children start to realise that when they make choices they should think about their responsibility to others and the environment. In the case of choosing alternative ways of getting to school, the children also have to consider their parents' opinions and discuss options with them.

### PAGES 10-11

The children could discuss how they choose to spend their money, especially if they are given money for a birthday or Christmas. Do they think about whether they need something and whether they can afford it? Do they consider whether there is something they need or want more? Do they ask advice from people or friends to find out if this is a good choice? This encourages them to form a strategy to help them make decisions. Discuss the idea of saving money. What would they save money for? Is there something they think the class, the school or their family should save for?

# Parents and Teachers

## PAGES 12-13
The children could compile their own lists or sets of favourite adverts and explain why they like them. To help them understand that advertisers target specific audiences, they could divide some adverts into those aimed at adults and those aimed at children. How are they different? Why? You could also discuss how advertisers persuade people to buy their products. There is a good handout for teachers from the Advertising Standards Authority website (http://www.asa.org.uk/asa/about/ Guided+Tours/Schools+and+Colleges).

## PAGES 14-15
You could ask the children to come up with a list of qualities that make a good friend. What are the most important qualities in a friend? They could discuss whether they have ever experienced peer pressure or used peer pressure to persuade a friend to do something. What phrases can we use to say no to someone? See also http://www.childline.org.uk/pdfs/Peer_ pressure_teach.pdf.

## PAGES 16-17
The idea of making choices to be safe and avoid risks links well with the previous peer pressure topic, as friends can often persuade children to take risks. Get the children to talk about what to do if they are not sure if something is safe or if they feel uncomfortable or under pressure.

## PAGES 18-19
Making choices about healthy eating links with making food choices from different countries and cultures (Unit 05: Living in a diverse world). Remind children that to make an informed choice they may need to research and find out more about a choice, so they may need to ask, read or look up on the Internet what constitutes a healthy choice of meal.

## Further Information

### BOOKS FOR CHILDREN
*Joe's Car (Thinkers series)* by Annabelle Dixon, illustrated by Tim Archbold (A&C Black, 2001)

*Dogger* by Shirley Hughes (Red Fox, 1993)

*Charlie's Checklist* by Rory S. Lerman, illustrated by Alison Bartlett (Macmillan Children's Books, 1997)

*The Scary Video (Thinkers series)* by Gill Rose, illustrated by Tim Archbold (A&C Black, 2001)

*The Sand Tray (Thinkers series)* by Don Rowe, illustrated by Tim Archbold (A&C Black, 2001)

### WEBSITES
http://www.askcedric.org.uk

http://www.childline.org.uk

http://www.nc.uk.net/esd (Education for Sustainable Development)

http://www.rospa.org.uk (Royal Society for the Prevention of Accidents)

## PAGES 20-21
Children could be given a particular dilemma and asked to draw a poster about the decision-making process they would use to help them make their choice. They could be asked to include the rights and responsibilities that should be considered for this choice, to use their imagination to understand how various other people might feel about the decision, and the potential consequences of their decision.

# Index